# CATS

## AN ANTHOLOGY
### ❧ OF ❧
## VERSE & PROSE

# CATS

## AN ANTHOLOGY
### ⤬ OF ⤬
## VERSE & PROSE

SMITHMARK

This edition published in 1994 by
SMITHMARK Publishers Inc.
16 East 32nd Street
New York
NY 10016

SMITHMARK books are available for bulk purchase for sales
promotion and for premium use. For details write or call
the manager of special sales, SMITHMARK Publishers Inc.
16 East 32nd Street, New York, 10016; (212) 532–6600

ISBN 0 8317 3827 8

Produced by Anness Publishing Limited
1 Boundary Row
London SE1 8HP

Printed and bound in Singapore by Star Standard

# Contents

*Chapter 1*

# THE HISTORICAL CAT

It is called in Hebrew *Catul*;
in Chaldean *Chatul*, pl. *Chatulin*;
in Greek *Katus*; in Latin *Catus* or *felis*;
in English the Cat.

From William Salmon,
*The English Physician* (1693)

When Noah took in the ark a pair of each of the animals, a male and a female, his followers said to him: "How are we and our cattle to live in peace and security while the lion is with us?" God therefore caused the lion to be seized and overpowered with fever, and that was the first occasion on which fever visited the earth, and that is why the lion is always in a state of fever. They next complained of the rat which, they said, would spoil their eatables, drinkables and goods. God therefore caused the lion to sneeze when there came forth from it the cat.

From *Hayat al-Hayawan*, a zoological lexicon, by Ad-Daniris

What happens when a house catches fire is quite extraordinary. Nobody makes any effort to put it out because only the cats are important. Everybody stands in a line trying to save the cats, but they slip past just the same and throw themselves into the flames. This distresses the Egyptians a great deal. All the people living in a house where a cat has died a natural death shave their eyebrows . . . Cats which have died are taken to Bubastis, where they are embalmed and buried in secret receptacles.

Herodotus, Greek historian
of the fifth century BC, describing
the customs of the Ancient Egyptians
in *The Histories*, Book I

The worth of a kitten from the night it is kittened until it shall open its eyes is a legal penny
And from that time, until it shall kill mice, two legal pence
And after it shall kill mice, four legal pence; and so it always remains.

From *The North Wales Code of Law* of Prince Howell
the Good, enacted in AD 936

Probably the first Englishwoman to be hanged
for witchcraft was Agnes Waterhouse. In 1566
she confessed to having sent her cat, who she
called Satan, to spoil butter, kill a neighbour's
livestock and bewitch a man to death. In return
for each of these deeds the cat is said to have
received one drop of Agnes' blood.

For twenty-five years an oral addition to standing orders of the native guard at Government House near Poona had been communicated regularly from one guard to another on relief, to the effect that any cat passing out of the front door was to be regarded as His Excellency the Governor and to be saluted accordingly. The meaning of this was that Sir Robert Grant, Governor of Bombay, died there in 1838 and on the day of his death a cat was seen to leave the house by the front door and walk up and down a particular path as it had been the Governor's habit to do after sunset. A Hindu sentry had observed this and mentioned it to others of his faith who made it a subject of superstitious conjecture, the result being that one of the priestly caste explained the mystery of the dogma of the transmigration of the soul from one body to another, and interpreted the circumstance to mean that the spirit of the deceased Governor had entered into one of the house pets. It was difficult to fix on a particular one, and it was therefore decided that every cat passing out from the main entrance after dark was to be treated with due respect and proper honours.

From Sir T E Gordon, *A Varied Life* (1907)

# Chapter 2

# THE LEGENDARY CAT

According to legend a cat has nine
lives. For three he plays, for three he strays,
and for the last three he stays.

Hear and attend and listen; for this befell and behappened and became and was, O my best beloved, when the Tame animals were wild. The Dog was wild, and the Horse was wild, and the Cow was wild, and the Sheep was wild, and the Pig was wild – as wild as wild could be – and they walked in the Wet Wild Woods by their wild lones. But the wildest of all the wild animals was the Cat. He walked by himself, and all places were alike to him.

From Rudyard Kipling (1865–1936),
*Just So Stories*

According to legend, Siamese cats have crossed eyes because they spent too long staring at the golden goblet of the Buddha.

The Turks believe, by I know not what tradition, that Mahomet loved his cat so well that, one day being consulted on some point of religion, he preferred to cut off the cuff of his sleeve on which that animal was sleeping than to wake it by rising to go and speak to the person awaiting him.

From the seventeenth-century French traveller
Tournefort's account of his journeys in the Near East

Greek legend says that Galinthia, princess of the city of Argos, was changed by the Fates into a cat, and that in that shape she served as high priestess to Hecate, the goddess of magic.

Freyja is the most renowned of the goddesses . . . When she goes on a journey she sits in a chariot drawn by two cats.

From Snorri Sturlson (1179–1241),
Icelandic poet, *The Prose Edda*

*March 11, Friday, 1791*

The Stiony on my right Eye-lid still swelled and inflamed very much. As it is commonly said that the Eye-lid being rubbed by the tail of a black Cat would do it much good if not entirely cure it, and having a black Cat, a little before dinner I made a trial of it, and very soon after dinner I found my Eye-lid much abated of the swelling and almost free from Pain.

From the Diary of the Reverend James
Woodforde (1740–1803)

Praise be to thee, O Ra, exalted Sekhem, thou art the Great Cat, the avenger of the gods and the judge of words and the president of the sovereign chiefs and the governor of the holy Circle; thou art indeed the bodies of the Great Cat.

From *The Seventy-five Praises of Ra*,
inscribed on the walls of royal tombs of
the XIX and XX Dynasties of
Thebes in Egypt

At Aix in Provence on the festival of Corpus Christi the finest tom-cat in the country, wrapped like a child in swaddling clothes, was publicly exhibited in a magnificent shrine. Every knee was bent, every hand strewed flowers or poured incense, and in short the cat on this occasion was treated like the god of the day.

From C Mills, *History of the Crusades* (1820)

# Chapter 3

# THE COMPANIONABLE CAT

I have a kitten, my dear, the drollest
of all creatures that ever wore a cat's skin.
Her gambols are not to be described and would
be incredible if they could. In point of
size she is likely to be a kitten always, being
extremely small for her age, but time I suppose
that spoils everything will make her
also a cat.

From a letter to Lady Hesketh
written by William Cowper
(1731–1800)

When the tea is brought at five o'clock,
And all the neat curtains are drawn with care,
The little black cat with bright green eyes
Is suddenly purring there.

At first she pretends, having nothing to do,
She has come in merely to blink by the grate,
But though tea may be late or the milk may be sour
She is never late.

From Harold Munro (1879–1932),
"Milk for the Cat"

It is a very inconvenient habit of kittens (Alice had once made the remark) that, whatever you say to them, they *always* purr. "If they would only purr for 'yes', and mew for 'no', or any rule of that sort," she had said, "so that one could keep up a conversation! But how *can* you talk with a person if they always say the same thing?"

From Lewis Carroll (1832–98), *Through the Looking-Glass*

For I will consider my Cat Jeoffry

For he is the servant of the Living God, duly and
     daily serving him.

For at the first glance of the glory of God in the East
     he worships in his way.

For this is done by wreathing body seven times
     round with elegant quickness.

For then he leaps up to catch the musk, which is the
     blessing of God upon his prayer.

For he rolls upon prank to work it in.

For having done duty and received blessing he
     begins to consider himself.

For this he performs in ten degrees.

For first he looks upon his fore-paws to see if they
     are clean.

For secondly he kicks up behind to clear away there.

For thirdly he works it upon stretch with
     fore-paws extended.

For fourthly he sharpens his paws by wood.

For fifthly he washes himself.

For sixthly he rolls upon wash.

For seventhly he fleas himself, that he may not be
     interrupted upon the beat.

For eighthly he rubs himself against a post.

For ninthly he looks up for his instructions.

For tenthly he goes in quest of food.

From Christopher Smart (1722–71), "Jubilate Agno"

All your wondrous wealth of hair;
Dark and fair,
Silken–shaggy, soft and bright
As the clouds and beams of night,
Pays my reverent hand's caress
Back with friendlier gentleness.

From Algernon Swinburne
(1837–1909), "To a Cat"

I shall never forget the indulgence with which
Dr Johnson treated Hodge his cat, for whom he
himself used to go out and buy oysters, lest the
servants, having that trouble, should take a
dislike to the poor creature.

From Boswell's *Life of Johnson* (1780)

Who's that ringing at my door bell?
A little pussy cat that isn't very well.
Rub its little nose with a little mutton fat,
That's the best cure for a little pussy cat.

D'Arcy Wentworth Thompson (1829–1902)

A cat came fiddling out of a barn
With a pair of bagpipes under her arm
She could sing nothing but Fiddle cum fee
The mouse has married the bumble bee
Pipe cat, dance mouse,
We'll have a wedding at our good house.

Anonymous nursery rhyme

Edward Lear, the nineteenth-century writer of humorous verse, was so fond of his tabby cat Foss, that when he moved house in San Remo, Italy, he had his second villa built as an exact replica of the first, purely to make sure that Foss felt at home.

*Quand je me joue à ma chatte, qui sait si elle passe son temps de moi plus que je ne fais d'elle?*

When I am playing with my cat, who knows whether she isn't amusing herself with me more than I am with her?

From Michael de Montaigne (1533–92), *Essays*, Book II

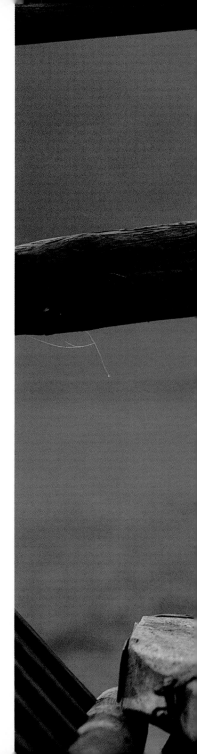

I and Pangur Ban, my cat,
'Tis a like task we are at;
Hunting mice is his delight
Hunting words I sit all night.

Oftentimes a mouse will stray
In the hero Pangur's way;
Oftentimes my keen thought set
Takes a meaning in his net.

From *Pangur Ban*, by an
unknown Irish monk and scribe
of the eighth century

# Chapter 4

# THE EVERLASTING CAT

I am the cat of cats, I am
The everlasting cat!
Cunning, and old, and sleek as jam,
The everlasting cat!
I hunt the vermin in the night –
The everlasting cat!
For I see best without the light –
The everlasting cat!

William Brightly Rands (1823–82)
"The Cat of Cats"

# THE CAT OF THE HOUSE

Over the hearth with my 'minishing eyes I muse
Until after
The last coal dies.
Every tunnel of the mouse,
Every channel of the cricket,
I have smelt.
I have felt
The secret shifting of the mouldered rafter,
And heard
Every bird in the thicket.
I see
You
Nightingale up in your tree!
I, born of a race of strange things,
Of deserts, great temples, great kings,
In the hot sands where the nightingale never sings!

Ford Madox Ford (1873–1939)

48

I can say with sincerity that I like cats . . . A cat is an animal which has more human feelings than almost any other.

From a letter by Emily Bronte (1818–48)

Slippers, the White House cat at the time of President Theodore Roosevelt, had the habit of going away, sometimes for weeks on end. But no matter how long he was absent he always returned in time for an important state dinner. Any person who wanted to know when such an occasion was about to take place had no need to consult the newspapers. If Slippers was sunning himself on the front steps that was a sure sign that the tables were being laid.

Cats are a mysterious kind of folk.
There is more passing in their minds than we
are aware of.

Sir Walter Scott (1771–1832)

Of all God's creatures there is only one
that cannot be made the slave of the lash. That
one is the cat. If man could be crossed with a
cat it would improve man, but it would
deteriorate the cat.

Mark Twain (1835–1910)

## THE CAT

Within that porch, across the way,
I see two naked eyes this night;
Two eyes that neither shut nor blink
Searching my face with a green light.
But cats to me are strange, so strange
I cannot sleep if one is near;
And though I'm sure I see those eyes,
I'm not sure a body's there.

W H Davies (1871–1940)

Cruel, but composed and bland
Dumb, inscrutable and grand,
So Tiberius might have sat,
Had Tiberius been a cat.

From Matthew Arnold (1822–88)
"Poor Mathias"

Cats when terrified stand at full height and arch their backs in a well-known and ridiculous fashion. They spit, hiss, or growl, the hair over the whole body, and especially on the tail, becomes erect.

From Charles Darwin (1809–82), *The Expression of the Emotions in Man and Animals*

O bard-like spirit! beautiful and swift!
Sweet lover of the pale night;
The dazzling glory of the gold-tinged tail,
Thy whisker-wavering lips!

Percy Bysshe Shelley (1792–1822)

It is a neat and cleanely creature, oftentimes licking his own body to keepe it smoothe and faire, having naturally a flexible backe for this purpose, and washing hir face with hir fore feet.

Edward Topsell, *Historie of Four-Footed Beastes*,
seventeenth century

See the kitten on the wall
Sporting with the leaves that fall,
Withered leaves – one – two – and three
From the lofty elder tree!
But the kitten, how she starts,
Crouches, stretches, paws and darts!
. . . What intenseness of desire
In her upward eye of fire.

From William Wordsworth
(1770–1850), "The Kitten and the
Falling Leaves"

Lat take a cat a fostre[1] hym wel with milk
And tendre flessh, and make his couche of silk,
And lay him seen a mous go by the wal,
Anon he weyveth[2] milk and flessh and al
And every deyntee[3] that is in that hous
Swich appetit hath he to ete a mous.

1 to nourish or feed
2 casts aside, forsakes
3 delicacy

From Geoffrey Chaucer (1343–1400),
*The Maunciple's Tale*

The cat is domestic only as far as suits its own ends; it will not be kennelled or harnessed nor suffer any dictations as to its goings out or comings in. Long contact with the human race has developed in it the art of diplomacy, and no Roman Cardinal of medieval days knew better how to ingratiate himself with his surroundings than a cat with a saucer of cream on its mental horizon.

From Saki (1870–1916), *The Square Egg*

# ACKNOWLEDGEMENTS

The Publishers would like to thank the following photographic libraries for their kind permission to reproduce their photographs:

Animal Photography / Sally Thompson 17, 21, 23, 27, 37, 53, 54, 55. Barnaby's Picture Library 15, 26, 35. Bruce Coleman / Jane Burton 1, 13, 14, 18, 19, 24, 30, 43, 56, 57, 60, 61. Bruce Coleman / Jane Burton & Kim Taylor 10. Bruce Coleman / Raimund Cramm GDT 44. Bruce Coleman / Eric Crichton 9. Bruce Coleman / Harald Lange 33. Bruce Coleman / Werner Layer 11. Bruce Coleman / Fritz Prenzel 25. Bruce Coleman / Mr Andy Price 22. Bruce Coleman / Hans Reinhard 2, 6, 8, 20, 38, 41, 45, 46, 49, 59, 63. Bruce Coleman / Uwe Walz 47. Sylvia Cordaiy / Paul Kaye 29. Sylvia Cordaiy / Monika Smith 51. Solitaire Photographic 42, 52. Spectrum Colour Library 12, 32, 34, 40, 50, 58.

*Edward Lear's drawing of his
adored cat, Foss.*